AF605674
N
W
E
S
QLD
QUEENSLAND
SA
SOUTH
AUSTRALIA
NSW
NEW SOUTH WALES
VIC
VICTORIA
ACT
AUSTRALIAN
CAPITAL
TERRITORY
TAS
TASMANIA

KYLE SURRY

KIDS' GUIDE TO AUSTRALIA'S STATES & TERRITORIES

DISCOVERING

QUEENSLAND

QLD

REDBACK publishing

First Published 2026 by
Redback Publishing
Suite 6, 13a Narabang Way,
Belrose NSW 2085
Australia

www.redbackpublishing.com
orders@redbackpublishing.com

ISBN 978-1-761400-63-6

Author: Kyle Surry
Editors: Lucinda Dodds and Emma Dobinson
Designer: Redback Publishing

MIX
Paper from responsible sources
FSC™ C001507

Original illustrations © Redback Publishing 2026
Originated by Redback Publishing

Acknowledgements
Abbreviations: l—left, r—right, b—bottom, t—top, c—centre, m—middle
We would like to thank the following for permission to reproduce photographs: (Images © shutterstock, Alamy) p7br - Contributor(s): Steele, J. G. (John Gladstone), 1935- - Item is held by John Oxley Library, State Library of Queensland, Public Domain, https://commons.wikimedia.org/w/index.php?curid=12655279, p12 - Maria Kazakova1 / Shutterstock.com, p13bl - Alex Cimbal / Shutterstock.com, p23r - Alex Cimbal / Shutterstock.com, p27tm - Squiresy92 including elements from Sodacan - Own work, CC BY-SA 4.0, https://commons.wikimedia.org/w/index.php?curid=48123007

NATIONAL LIBRARY OF AUSTRALIA
A catalogue record for this book is available from the National Library of Australia

CONTENTS

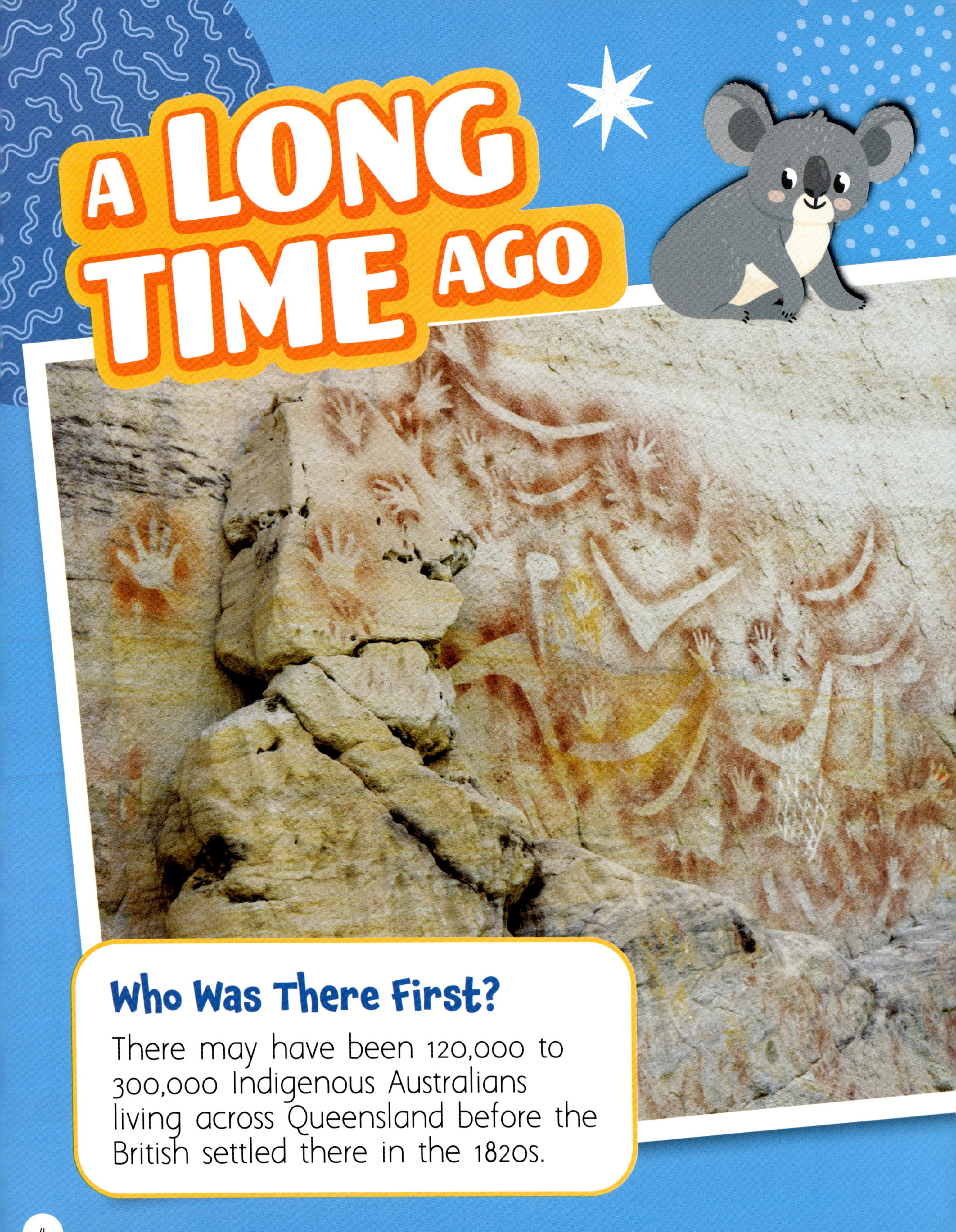

A LONG TIME AGO

Who Was There First?

There may have been 120,000 to 300,000 Indigenous Australians living across Queensland before the British settled there in the 1820s.

Rock art on cave walls in the Carnarvon Gorge is thousands of years old. On the walls of the caves are pictures of hands, boomerangs, people and animals.

Torres Strait Islands

The Torres Strait Islands were taken by Britain as part of the colony of Queensland in 1879. Ancestors of the Torres Strait Islanders had lived there for at least 8,000 years.

THE BRITISH ARRIVE

Timeline

1770 - Captain Cook named Moreton Bay as his ship sailed past it

1788 - All of Queensland was claimed by Britain and included as part of the colony of New South Wales

1824 - A very harsh convict settlement was built at Moreton Bay, which is now the site of the city of Brisbane

1859 - Queensland became a separate colony and was no longer a part of New South Wales

1901 - Federation made the colony of Queensland a state of Australia

Drawing of prisoner barracks

WHERE IS QUEENSLAND?

Queensland is the second largest state of Australia. It is in the northeast of Australia. Queensland has an area of 1.8 million square kilometres. It is about three times as big as France.

Where are the borders of Queensland?

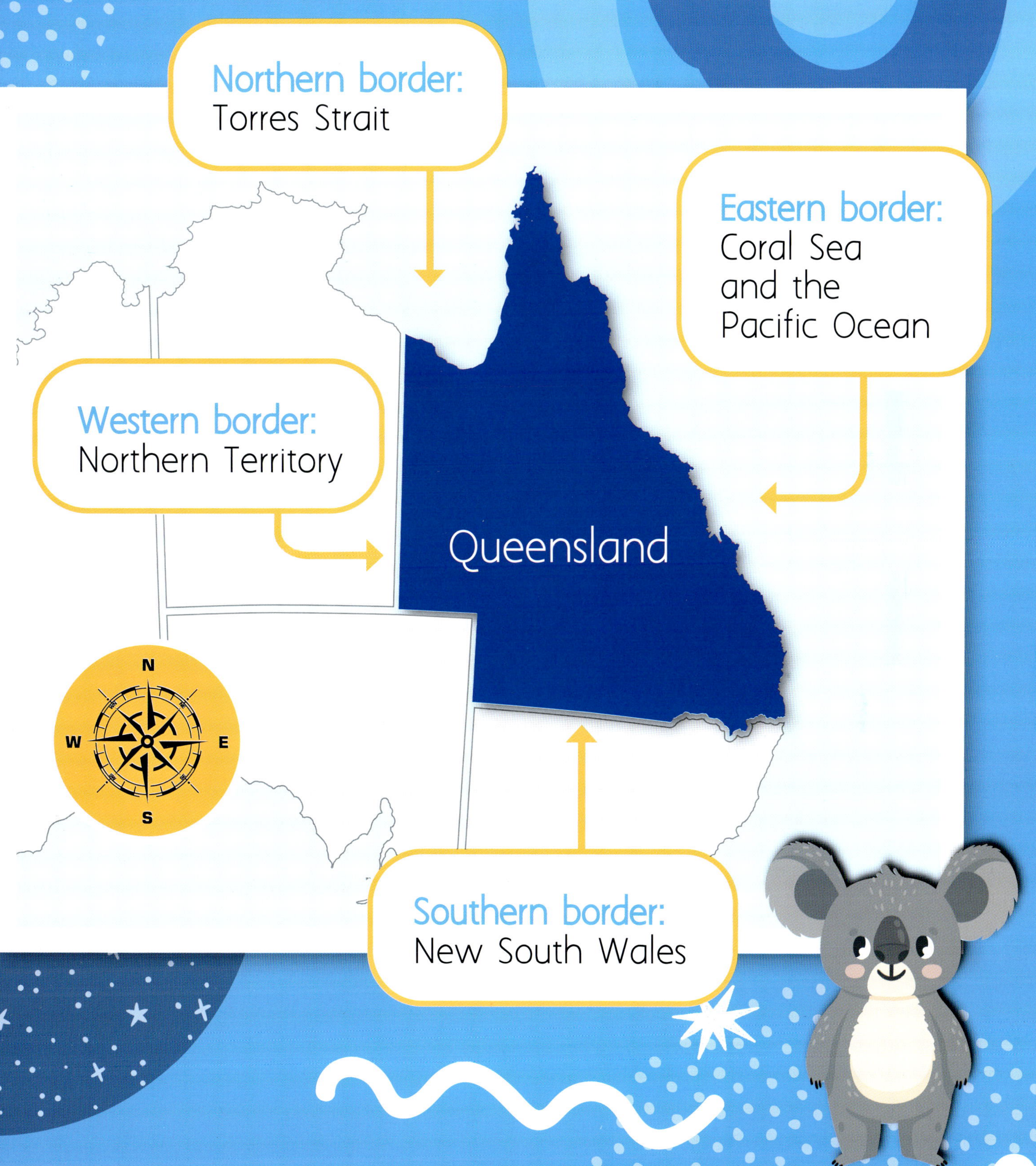

HOW MANY PEOPLE?

There are about 5.6 million people living in Queensland.

(ABS 2024)

About 23% of people in Queensland were born overseas, mostly in New Zealand, England, India or China.

Beyond the main towns in Queensland, there are deserts, rainforests and grassland where very few people live.

(ABS 2021)

Half the people in Queensland live in or near Brisbane.

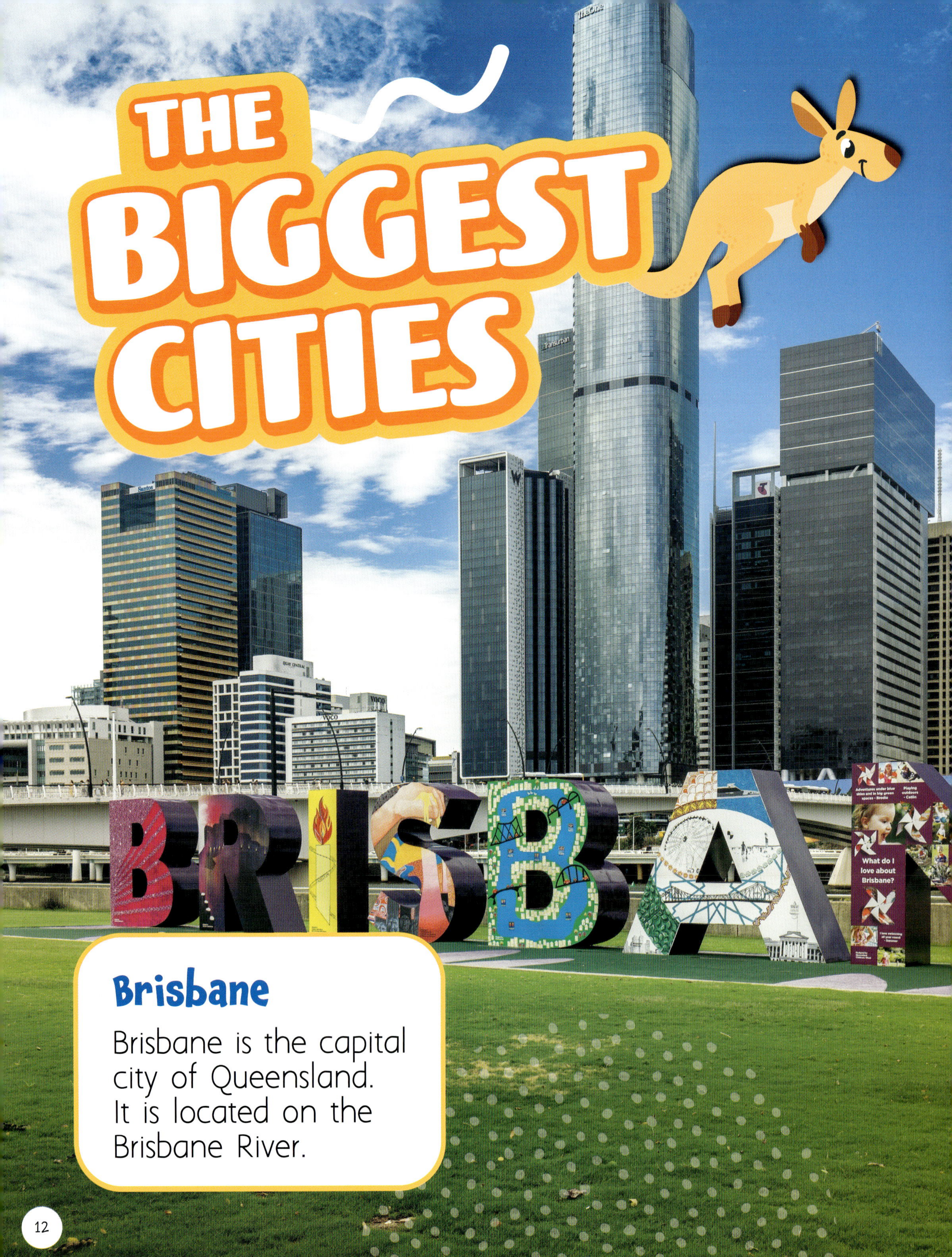

THE BIGGEST CITIES

Brisbane

Brisbane is the capital city of Queensland. It is located on the Brisbane River.

Townsville

Located on the coast of northeast Queensland, Townsville has a tropical climate.

Cairns

On the northern coast of Queensland, Cairns is close to the Great Barrier Reef.

Toowoomba

Toowoomba is the biggest inland town in Queensland.

THE LAND AND SEA

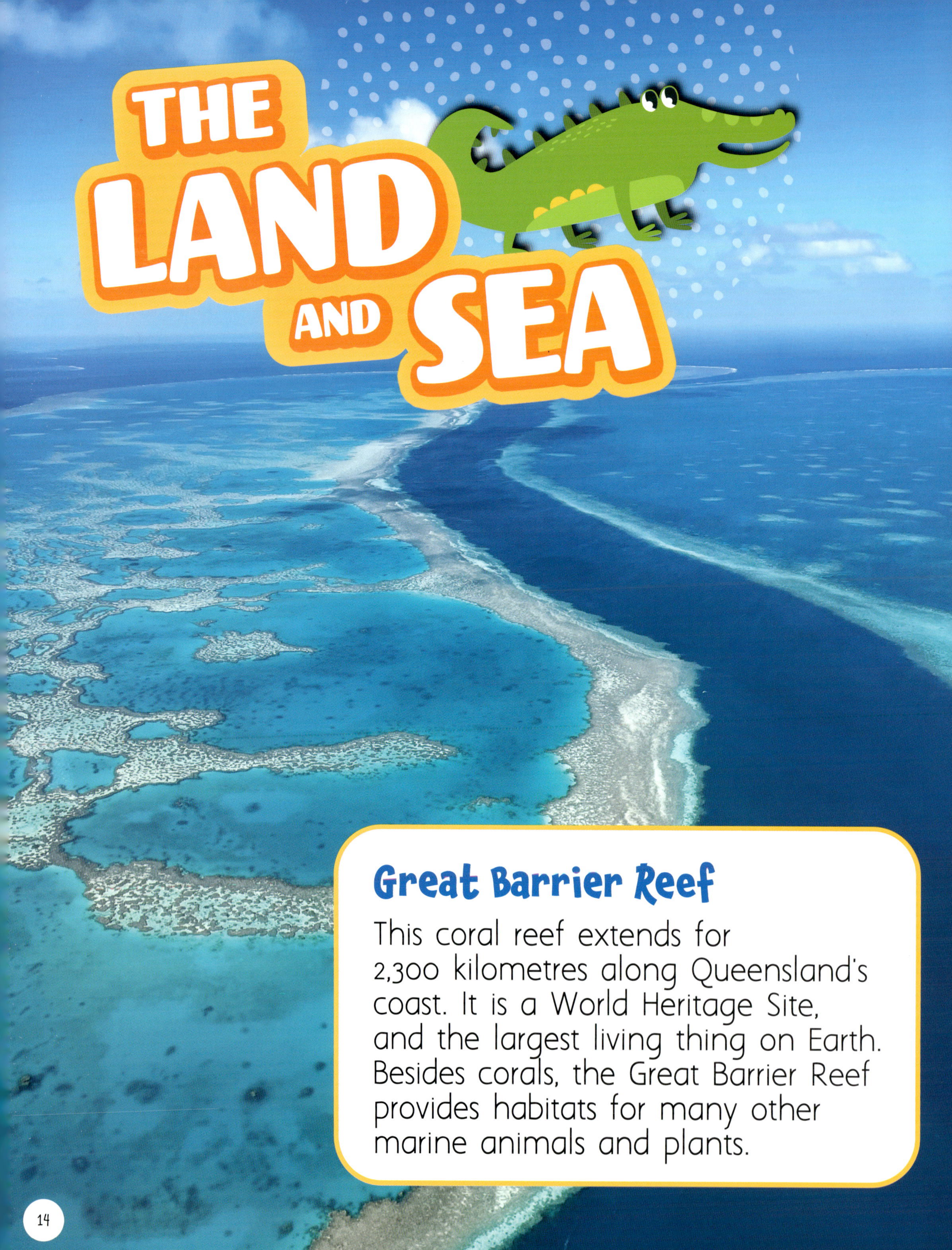

Great Barrier Reef

This coral reef extends for 2,300 kilometres along Queensland's coast. It is a World Heritage Site, and the largest living thing on Earth. Besides corals, the Great Barrier Reef provides habitats for many other marine animals and plants.

Great Dividing Range

This mountain range runs the whole length of Queensland. It separates the tropical coastline from the arid areas in the west of Queensland.

Gulf of Carpentaria

This is a large marine area. It has Cape York Peninsula on the east, and Arnhem Land in the Northern Territory on the west.

QUEENSLAND'S ISLANDS

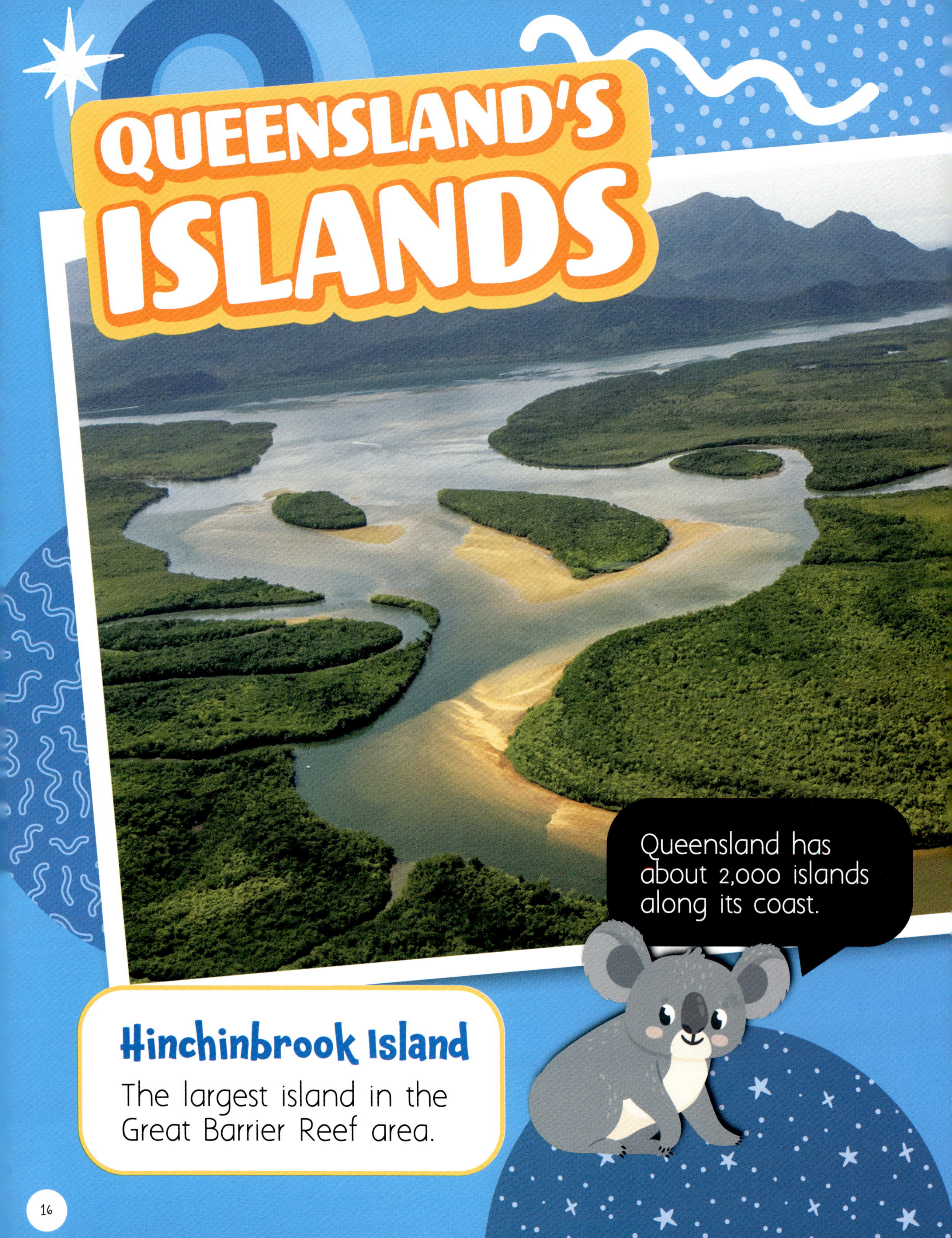

Hinchinbrook Island

The largest island in the Great Barrier Reef area.

Thursday Island

This is where the government for the Torres Strait Islands is located.

Magnetic Island

Captain Cook gave this island its name back in 1770.

Whitsunday Islands

Beautiful islands that are well-known for their tourist spots.

K'gari (Fraser Island)

This is the biggest sand island in the world.

RIVERS IN QUEENSLAND

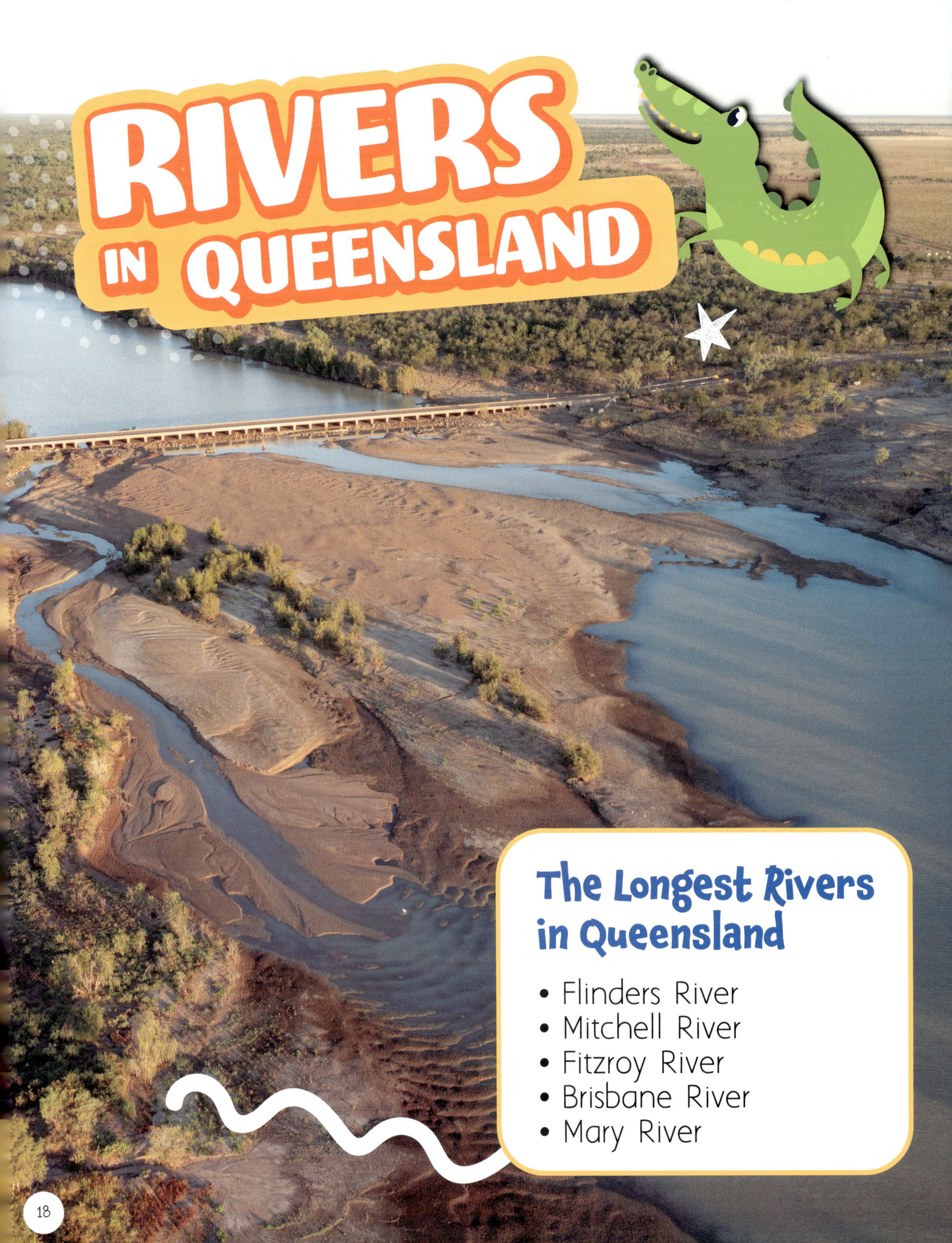

The Longest Rivers in Queensland

- Flinders River
- Mitchell River
- Fitzroy River
- Brisbane River
- Mary River

DESERTS IN QUEENSLAND

The deserts in Queensland are home to many plants and animals that can live in extreme conditions. Deserts are hot and there is very little water during the dry season.

Simpson Desert

This desert is a national park. It can only be crossed in the dry season.

Strzelecki Desert

Named after a Polish explorer.

Sturt Stony Desert

A gibber desert that is covered in small stones.

MINING

Coal

Coal is one of Queensland's biggest exports.

Aluminium

The area around Weipa is the main source of Queensland's aluminium ore.

Natural Gas

Before being exported, gas is turned into a liquid called LNG. It is then sent in special tanker ships.

Mount Isa

The massive deposits of minerals in the area around the town of Mount Isa include silver, lead, copper and zinc.

STATE GOVERNMENT

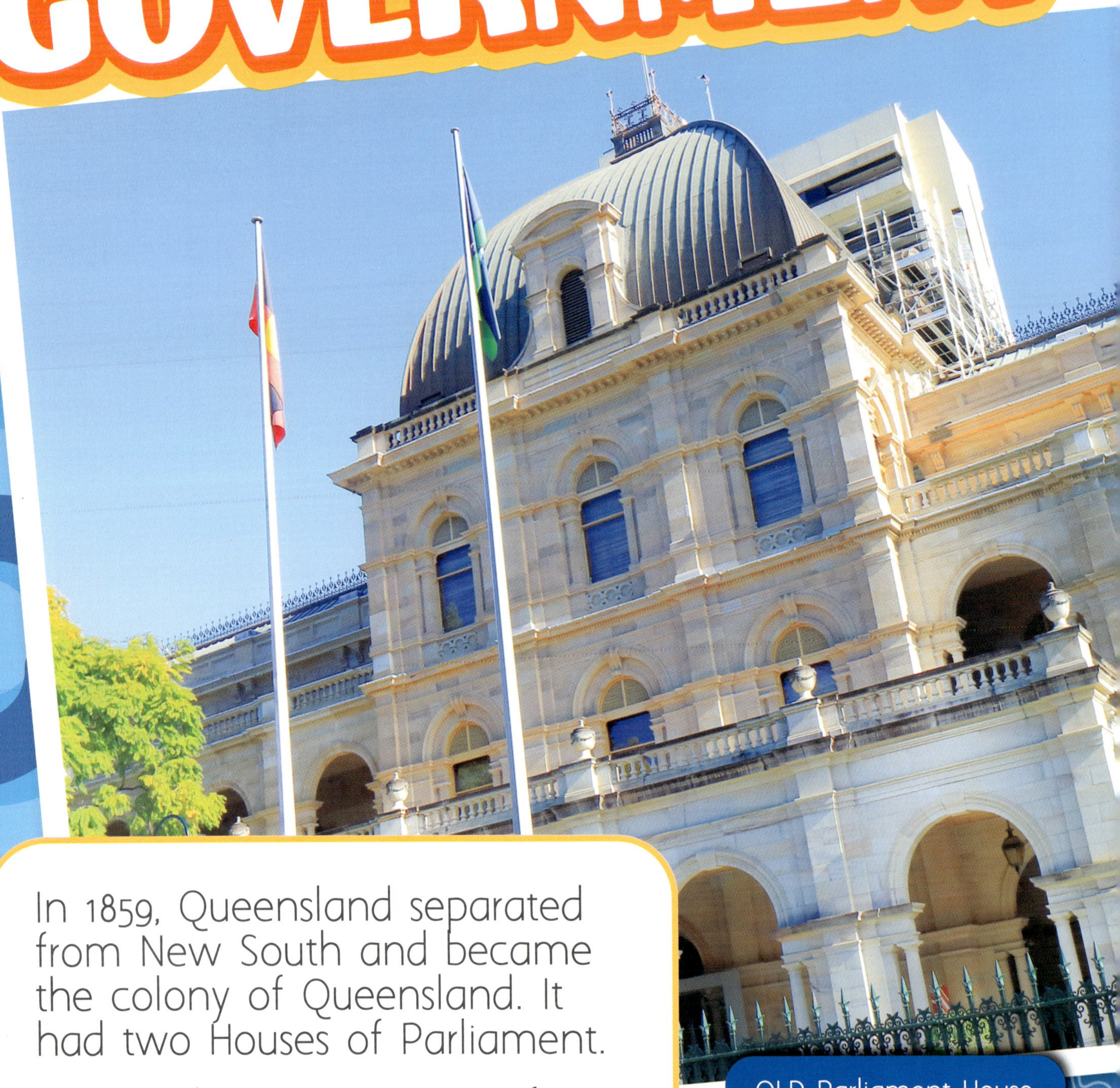

In 1859, Queensland separated from New South and became the colony of Queensland. It had two Houses of Parliament.

In 1922, the Upper House of Parliament was removed.

QLD Parliament House

Today, there is only one section, or House, in the Queensland Parliament. This is the Legislative Assembly, and it has 93 elected members.
Legislative Assembly chamber at Parliament House
Queensland is now the only state of Australia to have just one House in its Parliament.

FLAGS OF QUEENSLAND

Australian Aboriginal Flag

The Aboriginal Flag was first flown in 1971. It was designed by elder Harold Thomas in 1970.

What the flag represents:

Yellow Disc	The Sun and yellow ochre
Red	The land
Black	The Aboriginal people of Australia

Queensland State Flag

The Queensland flag was first used in 1876. The Union Jack is a reminder of Queensland's connection with Britain.

The Torres Strait Flag

This flag dates from 1992. It was designed by Bernard Namok.

White dhari (headdress)
A symbol of the Torres Strait Islanders

White five-pointed star
Symbolises peace and the five major island groups

Green stripes
The land

Black stripes
The people

Blue
The sea

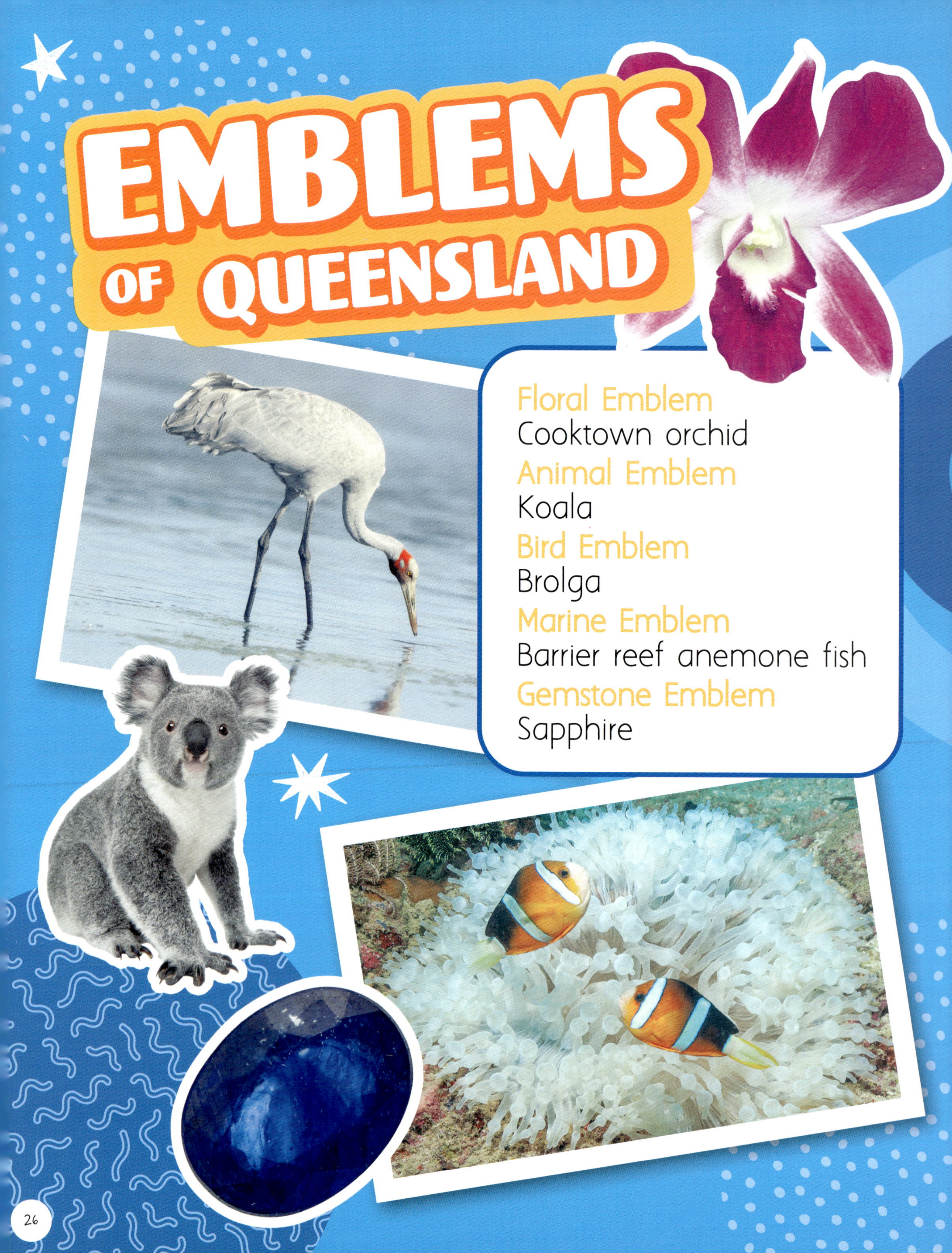

EMBLEMS OF QUEENSLAND

Floral Emblem
Cooktown orchid

Animal Emblem
Koala

Bird Emblem
Brolga

Marine Emblem
Barrier reef anemone fish

Gemstone Emblem
Sapphire

The Coat of Arms

This is a symbol of Queensland, and each part of it has a meaning:

Crest
Sugarcane

Red deer
Queen Victoria gave Queensland a herd of deer

Brolga
The bird emblem

Ram's head
The sheep industry

Bull's head
The cattle industry

Wheat
The wheat industry

Column of gold, rising from quartz
The mining industry

Motto
Audax at Fidelis which are Latin words meaning 'Bold but Faithful'.

GROWING SUGAR

Most of the sugar we use in Australia comes from sugarcane grown in Queensland. Most of the sugar grown on Queensland farms is sent to other countries.

Sugarcane grows along the east coast of Queensland, from Grafton to Mossman.
Sugarcane supports many country towns by providing jobs.

CANE TOADS

Cane toads were released into the sugarcane fields in 1935 to control the beetles that were destroying the crop.

The cane toad is slowly hopping across all of northern Australia.

The cane toad is now a terrible pest that poisons native animals and pets when they try to eat it.

GLOSSARY

ancestors people from the past who are related to those alive today

arid having a very low rainfall

capital city city where there is the government and is the main business centre of a state or country

colony settlement of people who move to a new country and impose their culture on it

elected chosen by people who vote

emblem image or design that symbolises something

exports products that a place sends to other places or countries

inland far away from the coast

Latin ancient language often used in science

settlers people who move to live in a different country, usually as farmers

symbol thing or image that represents something else

tropical climate climate that is hot and wet

World Heritage Site important place listed by the United Nations

INDEX

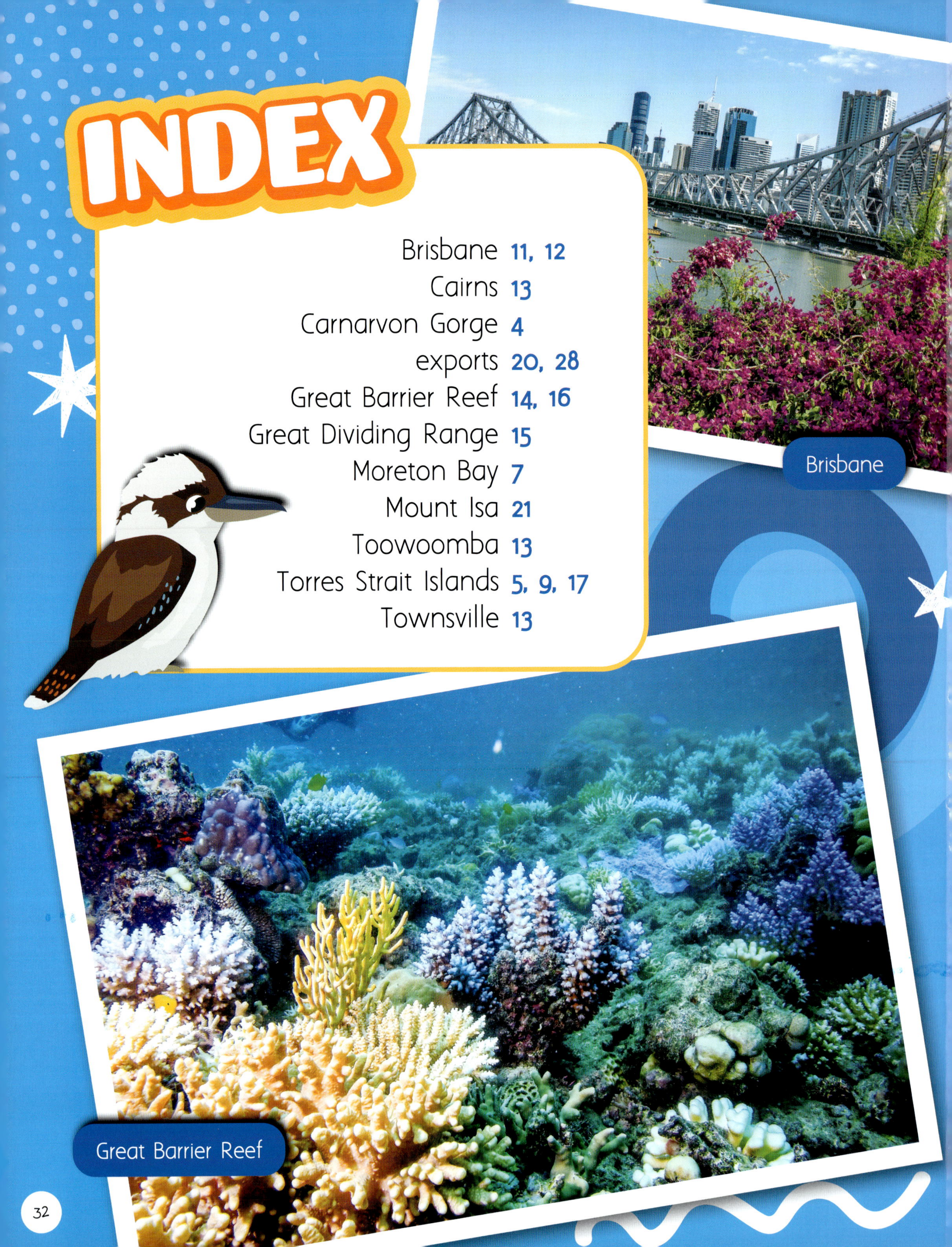

Brisbane

Great Barrier Reef

KIDS' GUIDE
TO
AUSTRALIA'S
STATES & TERRITORIES
NT
NORTHERN
TERRITORY
WA
WESTERN
AUSTRALIA